CRICKET

It's A Funny Old Game

CRICKET

It's A Funny Old Game

**ANDREW JOHN
AND
STEPHEN BLAKE**

Michael O'Mara Humour

First published in Great Britain in 2004 by
Michael O'Mara Books Limited
9 Lion Yard
Tremadoc Road
London SW4 7NQ

A CIP catalogue record for this book is available from
the British Library

ISBN 1-84317-090-6

1 3 5 7 9 10 8 6 4 2

Designed and typeset by Design 23

Printed and bound in England by Cox & Wyman Ltd,
Reading, Berks

Contents

Introduction

In cricket, there's funny and funny: you know, funny ha-ha and funny peculiar. Although it's a game played and loved all over the world, it always seems to conjure up all that's British – especially English. While you do get some belly laughs from cricket quotations, notably from commentators such as Henry Blofeld and Brian Johnston and characters such as Fred Trueman, you find most that is said is redolent of that air of British reserve and understatement with its dash of eccentricity.

In which other sport would you have a commentator taking a break from bringing us a ball-by-ball account of the action to say that a bumble bee has flown into the commentary box (and that he likes bumble bees, and ladybirds, too), or that a seagull – a winking seagull, no less – has just flown overhead? Yes, that's Henry Blofeld, the butterfly-brained, plummy-voiced commentator known and loved by cricket enthusiasts everywhere. It's a game that, like soccer, has its fair share of pundits. Indeed, as Fred Trueman says in these pages, 'If there is a game that attracts the half-baked theorists more than cricket, I've yet to hear of it.'

Yet those for whom a love of cricket is as strong as a love of life itself, you sense the awe in which they hold the game. And some of them bring their literary powers to bear to great effect, as Alistair

Cooke does elsewhere in this book, when he speaks of 'the smell of the dandelions, the puff of the pipe, the click of the bat, the rain on the neck, the chill down the spine, the slow, exquisite coming on of sunset and dinner and rheumatism'. We assume he's referring to village cricket there, which holds as great an affection in the nation's heart as the game at county or Test level. And you'll find a number of choice quotations among this collection to sum up those sentiments.

Enjoy reading what cricketers, commentators, players of other sports and even a few spectators have had to say about this most cherished game. We hope you'll nod in agreement at some of the heartfelt verbal homage and find some gems to get you laughing – especially in the section devoted to gaffes and trips of the tongue.

Even works of compilation require the loving care of an editor, and we thank Helen Cumberbatch of Michael O'Mara Books for her unstinting help and guidance.

So, if you like what you read, try our companion volume, *Football: It's A Funny Old Game*.

Andrew John and Stephen Blake
Spring 2004

From the pitch to the pavilion

Whether it's cricketers talking about other cricketers or cricketers talking about themselves, the following quotes are all views aired by a variety of characters from the cricketing world about players, clubs, captains and coaches.

I don't go as far as that on my *holidays.*

FORMER BOWLER ON HOW FAR BOB WILLIS USED TO
RUN UP TO THE WICKET FOR HIS DELIVERY

People no longer ask me if he advises me, because it's obvious that he doesn't – or if he does then I'm taking no notice.

CHRIS COWDREY ON HIS FAMOUS FATHER

A conversation with him would be fifty per cent shorter if he deleted the expletives.

MIKE SELVEY ON JOHN EMBUREY

[Angus] Fraser's approach to the wicket currently resembles someone who has his braces caught in the sightscreen.

MARTIN JOHNSON

[Angus] Fraser reminds me of my favourite things: aeroplanes. His bowling's like shooting down F-16s with sling shots. Even if they hit, no damage would be done. Like an old horse, he should be put out to pasture.

COLIN CROFT

[Graeme] Hick is just a flat-track bully.

JOHN BRACEWELL

Cricket in Yorkshire is not as it is elsewhere. It never has been. The club has always been a battleground between warring factions. Civil war is never far below the surface of Yorkshire cricket.

JAMES P. COLDHAM

A natural mistimer of the ball.

ANGUS FRASER ON MIKE ATHERTON
(QUOTED BY ATHERTON HIMSELF)

He's a show pony. He's a prima donna. [Dominic] Cork may have talent, but he does have an attitude problem. If you think *I* was bad, my God, he's three times worse.

GEOFF BOYCOTT

At times he looks as though he has an artificial brain, slightly out of tune with his body.

CHRISTOPHER MARTIN-JENKINS ON GRAEME HICK

Eeyore without the *joie de vivre*.

MIKE SELVEY ON ANGUS FRASER

If someone wore a chocolate bar on his head, Goughie would follow suit.

STEVE OLDHAM ON DARREN GOUGH
(AND HIS LOVE OF GIMMICKS)

He's a hard beggar and he has a strong mind.

RAY ILLINGWORTH ON MIKE ATHERTON

Sometimes it takes him a fortnight to put on his socks.

MICKY STEWART ON DEVON MALCOLM
(AND HIS LAID-BACK MANNER)

They really are a bunch of twits. According to them I was crap. We didn't gel at all. I was opposed because of my Calvin Klein underwear; I was opposed for wearing certain clothes; and I was opposed because I didn't drink.

CHRIS LEWIS ON HIS TIME AT NOTTINGHAMSHIRE CCC

Almost as good a bullsh**ter as Bob Woolmer.

A WARWICKSHIRE INSIDER ON DERMOT REEVE

Why go to the nets for two hours when all your mates are down the kebab house making career-best scores on the Galactic Defender?

PHIL TUFNELL

The enigma with no variation.

VIC MARKS ON CHRIS LEWIS

I don't like you, Reeve. I never have liked you. You get right up my nose, and if you come anywhere near me I'll rearrange yours.

DAVID LLOYD TO DERMOT REEVE
(QUOTED BY REEVE)

The other advantage England have got when Phil Tufnell's bowling is that he isn't fielding.

IAN CHAPPELL

ON GEOFF BOYCOTT

This can only help England's cause.

IAN BOTHAM, WHEN GEOFF BOYCOTT WAS GIVEN A TWO-
WEEK JOB OF COACHING YOUNG PAKISTANI BATSMEN

The greatest tragedy of his troubled life is that,
above all else, in the desire to be admired and loved
by everyone, he has this enormous capacity for
upsetting people.

TONY GREIG

You cannot motivate a team with the word 'I'. Geoff
[Boycott] cannot fool anyone: they know he's totally,
almost insanely, selfish.

IAN BOTHAM

Geoffrey [Boycott] is the only fellow I've met who
fell in love with himself at a young age and has
remained faithful ever since.

DENNIS LILLEE (SAID IN JEST)

ON IAN BOTHAM

You should have stuck to soccer, lad.

LEN MUNCER, COACH, ON BOTHAM'S CRICKET PROSPECTS

Ian [Botham] is a man who is very warm in friendship, but very ugly in enmity.

PETER ROEBUCK

He's like a big soft puppy, really.

TOM CARTWRIGHT

I'm aware he smokes dope – but doesn't everyone?

TIM HUDSON ON IAN BOTHAM IN 1986
(HE WAS SUBSEQUENTLY SACKED AS BOTHAM'S AGENT)

If you made him prime minister tomorrow, he'd pick this country up in ten minutes.

BILL ALLEY, UMPIRE

He couldn't bowl a hoop downhill.

FRED TRUEMAN

[Ian] Botham's idea of team spirit and motivation was to squirt a water pistol at someone and then go and get pissed.

RAY ILLINGWORTH

Ian Botham would make a great Aussie.

JEFF THOMSON

He doesn't give a damn; he wants to ride a horse, down a pint, roar around the land, waking up the sleepers, show them things can be done. As it is, he has to play cricket all the time, and worry about newspapermen, a Gulliver tied down by the little people.

PETER ROEBUCK

ON DAVID GOWER

Perhaps [David] Gower will eventually realize that cricket's not always about champagne: it's a bread-and-butter game.

BRIAN BRAIN

Difficult to be more laid back without being actually comatose.

FRANCES EDMONDS (WIFE OF THE SPIN BOWLER, PHIL)

A master in the art of non-communication.

GEOFF BOYCOTT ON GOWER AS CAPTAIN

The new Briton – forceful, plebeian, undeferential, a winner. He is cricket's Thatcher.

SUNDAY TELEGRAPH JOURNALIST ON GRAHAM GOOCH

The face of a choirboy, the demeanour of a civil servant and the ruthlessness of a rat catcher.

GEOFF BOYCOTT ON DEREK UNDERWOOD

Don't swat those flies, Jardine, they're the only friends here you've got.

YABBA, A SPECTATOR, TO DOUGLAS JARDINE, WHO HAD WAVED HIS HAND TO SWAT A FLY FROM HIS FACE

I'd rather face Dennis Lillee with a stick of rhubarb than go through all that again.

IAN BOTHAM, AFTER BEING CLEARED OF ASSAULT IN 1981

If [Tony] Greig fell off the Empire State Building, he'd land on a furniture van full of mattresses.

AN ANONYMOUS ENGLAND TEAMMATE

That load of madmen will never win anything until they learn some self-discipline.

RAY ILLINGWORTH ON ESSEX IN THE 1970S, BEFORE THEY WENT ON TO WIN EVERYTHING

Of all the left-armers I have faced on a wet, helpful pitch, Derek [Underwood] was the closest to being unplayable.

TREVOR BAILEY

A 1914 biplane tied up with elastic bands trying vainly to take off.

FRANK KEATING ON BOB WILLIS

England players have a typical English-like attitude, which is different than Pakistani attitude.

KRIS SRIKKANTH

There's only one head bigger than [Tony] Greig's – and that's Birkenhead.

FRED TRUEMAN

That Randall! He bats like an octopus with piles.

AN ANONYMOUS SOUTH AUSTRALIAN,
SAID OF DEREK RANDALL

All right, this bloke's a prime candidate for a run out – he's a bit fat and he's wearing rubber soles.

PETER BICKLE

England players traditionally have been playing very traditional cricket.

KRIS SRIKKANTH

You write anything bad about me and I'll come and whack you. It's time someone was sorted out. I'll start with you. I'll be checking this out. Be careful.

VIV RICHARDS TO A JOURNALIST

I couldn't stand the Birmingham accent.

JOHN EMBUREY ON JUSTIFYING HIS DECISION TO TURN
DOWN THE CHANCE TO CAPTAIN WARWICKSHIRE

Surrey is run as a regime of fear and secrecy. It is no longer a members' club. It is more influenced by the 'Meet John Major' syndrome.

PAUL AMES, SECRETARY OF THE
SURREY ACTION GROUP IN 1995

There are too many old men in English cricket . . . these are the men who are stopping the young players coming through.

ASIF IQBAL IN 1983

Perhaps I don't have enough initials – it's a handicap only having two.

TREVOR JESTY, ON BEING PASSED OVER FOR THE
HAMPSHIRE CAPTAINCY IN FAVOUR OF
M. C. J. NICHOLAS IN 1985

I've lost more good players through interfering parents than for any other reason.

COLIN PAGE, COACH

County cricketers are a cautious lot. Though they've scored runs throughout their careers, they do not trust to luck. They construct a technique in which imagination plays no part. Everything is tight, everything is predictable.

PETER ROEBUCK

The typical 1990s cricketer was a decent, regular middlebrow man who read the *Daily Mail* and Wilbur Smith novels and (except in Lancashire) dressed at C&A.

SIMON HUGHES

Most of us were technically better at fourteen than we are now.

PETER ROEBUCK ON COUNTY CRICKET

When it comes to moaning, he's world-class.

KIM BARNETT ON CHRIS ADAMS IN 1998

Don't give advice to a batsman going in: if he's inexperienced, it will only make him nervous; if he is an old hand, it is generally unnecessary. Give him credit and opportunity to use his own judgement; if he doesn't do so at first, he soon will.

GILBERT JESSOP IN 1929

They [the old pros] tended to enjoy horse racing, and the suspension of play due to rain. Without any doubt the best hours of the day for them were spent in the pub after the day's play.

IMRAN KHAN IN 1988

He looks like a cuddly little panda.

TONY BROWN ON MIKE GATTING, AFTER THE LATTER
SUFFERED A NOSE INJURY

The vast majority of county cricketers have two topics of conversation: 'Me and My Cricket', or, as a high-day and holiday variant, 'My Cricket and Me'.

FRANCES EDMONDS

County bowlers are nothing if not philosophical. I'll be there in midsummer, running up to Sir Geoffrey, convincing myself he's going to pad up to a straight one.

BRIAN BRAIN

Most county cricketers play the game for the life rather than the living. For them it's the motorways of England rather than the jet lanes of the world. It's sausage, egg and chips at Watford Gap rather than vol-au-vents and small talk on the governor-general's lawn in Barbados.

MICHAEL CAREY

Mandela's first words to me were, 'Fraser, can you please tell me, is Donald Bradman still alive?'

MALCOLM FRASER, AUSTRALIAN PRIME MINISTER

A snick by Jack Hobbs is a sort of disturbance of cosmic orderliness.

NEVILLE CARDUS

Like a meteor which flashes across the sky, creating an unforgettable impression and then vanishing, so Frank [Tyson] burst on to the first-class cricket scene.

FRED TRUEMAN

Cricketers are found almost everywhere that the English language is spoken; as well as in Yorkshire and Lancashire. They are not of course found in America – which explains a lot!

CARDEW ROBINSON

Spectators who did not fall asleep before tea at the Saffrons yesterday were undoubtedly kept awake by the town hall clock, which, for much of the time, was striking more frequently than the Sussex batsmen.

DOUG IBBOTSON, DAILY TELEGRAPH

A cricket ball is a shining miracle of leather, cork and twine, but when dispatched by a bat swung by a Bonner or a Dexter it becomes a missile of enormous power and speed.

GERALD BRODRIBB

There is a myth that when Yorkshire cricket prospers, peace breaks out in the county of the broad acres; but history shows that Yorkshire cricket has to be at peace with itself for it to prosper.

JAMES P. COLDHAM

We are all Adam's children – it's just the silk that makes all the difference.

NAVJOT SIDHU

To change a Brett Lee or a Allan Donald would be nearly impossible. I know Tiger Woods changed his golf swing, but he is a freak.

DR RICHARD STRETCH OF THE UNITED CRICKET BOARD OF
SOUTH AFRICA ON THE DIFFICULTY OF CHANGING A
BOWLER'S ACTION

Venkatesh Prasad, don't get upset because I upset you, take it cool.

KRIS SRIKKANTH

We make a good pair, don't we? I can't f**king bat and you can't f**king bowl.

ROBIN SMITH TO MERV HUGHES AFTER THE LATTER HAD SUGGESTED THAT THE FORMER WAS A HOPELESS BATSMAN, AND SMITH HAD THEN HIT HUGHES FOR SIX

INTERVIEWER: What's your favourite animal?
STEVE WAUGH: Merv Hughes.

INTERVIEWER: Do you feel that the selectors and yourself have been vindicated by the result?
MIKE GATTING: I don't think the press are vindictive. They can write what they want.

Hogg suggested we survey the back of the Adelaide Oval, and I don't think he had a tennis match on his mind.

GRAHAM YALLOP ON A DIFFERENCE OF OPINION WITH HIS TEAMMATE RODNEY HOGG

He was my first England captain, my first England opening partner, he stands next to me and bores the pants off me at slip – he's a great guy.

MARK BUTCHER ON MIKE ATHERTON

He is a dibbly-dobbly bowler.

NAVJOT SIDHU

GREG THOMAS, BOWLING TO VIV RICHARDS, WHO HAD
MISSED A SUPERB OUT-SWINGER: It's red, round and
weighs about five and a half ounces.
RICHARDS, HAVING THEN HIT THOMAS OUT OF THE
GROUND: Greg, you know what it looks like. Go ahead
and find it!

A call for a run from Bob Blanchard is not so much
a statement of intent but more a basis for
negotiation.

MARK PULLING

RAMAN SUBBA ROW, AFTER LETTING THE BALL GO
BETWEEN HIS LEGS: 'I should've kept my legs together,
Fred.'
FRED TRUEMAN'S REJOINDER: 'Not you, son. Your
mother should've!'

I knocked his helmet straight off his head. It went to
pieces and blood came out . . . I thought it was brains
coming out. I think he was pretty happy to be alive.

JEFF THOMSON ON THE FIRST TIME HE BOWLED
TO MARTIN CROWE OF NEW ZEALAND

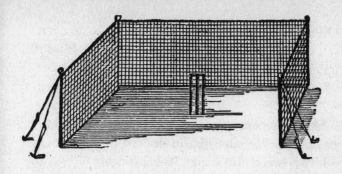

Have nothing to do with coaches. In fact, if you
should see one coming, go and hide behind the
pavilion until he goes away.

BILL O'REILLY

If there were twenty-two Trevor Baileys playing in a
match, who would ever go and watch it?

ARTHUR MORRIS

I used to think cricket was fun. Then I saw Ken
Norling bat.

CHRIS HANSEN

He is like a one-legged man in a bum-kicking
competition.

NAVJOT SIDHU (SUBJECT OF THE COMMENT IS UNKNOWN)

I might be a s**t cricketer, but I'm a s**t cricketer in
a premiership team.

DAVE NADEL

Off the field, he could be your life-long buddy, but out in the middle he had all the lovable qualities of a demented rhinoceros.

COLIN MCCOOL ON BILL O'REILLY

There is, of course, a world of difference between cricket and the movie business . . . I suppose doing a love scene with Racquel Welch roughly corresponds to scoring a century before lunch.

OLIVER REED

The selectors are full of s**t.

CHRIS LEWIS NOT HAPPY ABOUT BEING
LEFT OUT OF A SIDE IN 1998

I thought you needed designer stubble to get into the England team these days.

MIKE GATTING, WHO HAD JUST SHAVED OFF
HIS BEARD IN 1993

These days a captain has to concentrate on making his players believe that they have the ability to succeed.

BOB WILLIS

I will never be accepted by the snob press.

RAY ILLINGWORTH IN 1973

AIR STEWARD: Would you like me to take anything home for you?

BOB WILLIS, THE ENGLAND CAPTAIN: Yes, thirty-four journalists and two camera crews.

As a county captain, one seems to spend an inordinate amount of time filling in forms of which no one takes the slightest notice.

RAY ILLINGWORTH

Captaincy seems to involve half-hearing conversations which you'd rather not hear at all.

PETER ROEBUCK

As captain you can never be one of the boys.

TONY LEWIS

I have often thought what a pity it is – how much
better a life I would have had, what a better man I
would have been, how much healthier an existence I
would have led, if I had been a cricketer instead of
an actor. But it was not to be.

LAURENCE OLIVIER

There is a final drop of venom which transforms a
good bowler into a great one.

T. C. F. PRITTIE

[A] successful cricket captain . . . needs the patience
of a saint, the diplomacy of an ambassador, the
compassion of a social worker and the skin of a rhino.

RAY ILLINGWORTH

Bowlers and wicket-keepers, however brilliant, cannot
by the nature of their work captivate the spectator in
quite the same way as the greatest batsman.

E. W. SWANTON

It has been said that bowlers, like poets, are not made.

I. A. R. PEEBLES

A true batsman should in most of his strokes tell the
truth about himself.

NEVILLE CARDUS

Great wicket-keepers are born and not made.

KEITH ANDREW

A batsman who cannot make runs on turf after rain and sun and wind is only half a batsman.

H. H. D. SEWELL

An Englishman's crease is 'is castle.

HUBERT PHILLIPS

Hell has no fury like a cricketer who fancies some slight has been made on his prowess.

R. T. JOHNSTON

I always felt very fortunate to be a professional cricketer, to be paid for doing something I loved and which was a hobby.

BOB TAYLOR

Why is [Phil] Tufnell the most popular man in the team? Is it the Manuel factor, in which the most helpless member of the cast is most affectionately identified with?

MIKE BREARLEY

If you were to ask a representative of almost any profession . . . what were the essential qualities of their calling, they would almost certainly say honesty, integrity and a sense of humour. In a good village cricket captain these qualities would be utterly redundant.

ROBERT HOLLES

At the 1996 World Cup, the England squad resembled a bad-tempered grandmother attending a teenage rave.

MATTHEW ENGEL

All the never-say-die qualities of a kamikaze pilot.

AUSTRALIAN JOURNALIST ON ENGLAND'S TEAM

They bring him out of the loft, take the dust sheet off him, give him a pink gin and sit him there. He can't go out of a thirty-mile radius of London because he's normally too pissed to get back. He sits there at Lord's saying, 'That Botham, look at his hair. They tell me he's had some of that cannabis stuff . . .'

IAN BOTHAM ON HIS VIEW OF THE
TYPICAL ENGLAND SELECTOR

If I were being polite, I'd say that Gatt is a little long in the tooth, somewhat immobile and carries too much weight. But I prefer straight talking, so I'm saying what I really think. Gatt is too old, too slow and too fat.

GEOFF BOYCOTT ON MIKE GATTING

He's not a motivator: he's just a whinger.

ALLAN LAMB ON RAY ILLINGWORTH

No longer should we allow international cricketers to appear on our television sets to be interviewed unshaven, chewing gum and altogether looking slovenly. These habits are to be deplored and should be eliminated.

LORD MACLAURIN, CHAIR OF THE ENGLAND
AND WALES CRICKET BOARD, 1998

I can remember some good Saturdays against the West Indies before – the only trouble is that the Thursdays, Fridays, Mondays and Tuesdays were a bit of a disaster.

JOHN EMBUREY

He crossed the line between eccentricity and idiocy far too often for someone who was supposed to be running English cricket.

IAN BOTHAM ON TED DEXTER

I wouldn't say I have reached the stage where I am going to tell the selectors to stuff it, but . . . I have got as far as saying sod 'em.

DAVID GOWER, AFTER NOT BEING RECALLED TO THE ENGLAND SQUAD

A fart competing with thunder.

GRAHAM GOOCH ASSESSING ENGLAND IN AUSTRALIA IN 1990–1

If I had my way, I would take him to the Traitors' Gate and personally hang, draw and quarter him.

IAN BOTHAM ON RAY ILLINGWORTH

The one-thousand-cc motorbike rider who came in like Lawrence of Arabia and went out like Mr Magoo.

MARTIN JOHNSON ON HOW THE PUBLIC PERCEIVED TED DEXTER

England have only three major problems: they can't bat, they can't bowl and they can't field.

MARTIN JOHNSON, *THE INDEPENDENT*

You're not too old to play cricket at thirty-five-plus. But you've got to be about sixty-plus if you want to administer the game or administer the team at international level. So you walk around a field for about twenty years and forget everything you've learned. It doesn't make any sense.

IAN BOTHAM

I'm not talking to anyone in the British media – they're all pricks.

ALLAN BORDER

No one has ever called me Future England Captain.
That was a media invention.

MIKE ATHERTON IN 1993

You should play every game as if it's your last, but
perform well enough to make sure it's not.

JOHN EMBUREY

He will see that trying to shake up English cricket is
like stirring dead sheep.

RAY ILLINGWORTH ON LORD MACLAURIN AS CHAIR OF THE
ENGLAND AND WALES CRICKET BOARD IN 1997

Old cricketers become bores.

DAVID FRITH

Only two problems with our team: brewer's droop
and financial cramp. Apart from that, we ain't
bloody good enough.

CHARLIE PARKER'S COMMENT ON LIFE AT
GLOUCESTERSHIRE IN THE 1920s

Simon Hughes thanks everyone who donated to
today's benefit collection, which raised one
thousand two hundred and thirty pounds, thirty
pence, seventy Canadian cents, fifty pesetas, one
Kenyan shilling and two Iranian shekels.

PUBLIC ANNOUNCEMENT AT LORD'S, 1991

Dear Mr Edrich, I would like you to know that, if I did want to have all my teeth extracted in one go, that is the way I wanted it done. Well played, Sir.

TIMES READER'S LETTER, PRINTED AFTER HE HAD BEEN HIT BY A BILL EDRICH SHOT WHILE READING HIS NEWSPAPER AT LORD'S IN 1938

It was hardly a heavyweight contest featuring the two hardest blokes on the county circuit – more like Spice Boy versus Spice Girl. I've already had my mum on the phone. She thinks I've committed some sort of crime against the state.

MARK ILOTT, AFTER A WELL-PUBLICIZED SPAT WITH ROBERT CROFT IN 1997

This is the last thing we need. He should not be entering nude pictures in magazine competitions. He is supposed to be an ambassador for Sussex County Cricket Club.

SUSSEX MEMBER ON NIGEL BETT'S PICTURE IN *BRITISH NATURISM*

All cricketers have large egos. That is why there are so many below-average players still in the game. Each player believes that he is a better cricketer than his results show.

PETER WALKER

Fast bowlers wearing earrings? I don't know what the game's coming to.

FRED TRUEMAN ON DEREK PRINGLE

When you have two workhorses and shoot them in the back, I think it's evil. You don't treat animals in this way. I was blindfolded, led up an alley and assassinated.

VIV RICHARDS, AFTER SOMERSET FAILED
TO RENEW HIS CONTRACT IN 1986

He may be good enough for England, but not for Yorkshire.

BRIAN SELLERS, AFTER YORKSHIRE HAD
SACKED JOHNNY WARDLE

F**king cheating c**t.

UMPIRE SHAKOOR RANA TO MIKE GATTING,
AFTER THE LATTER HAD MOVED ONE OF
HIS FIELDERS DURING A TOUR OF PAKISTAN

If you get one F, give two Fs back.

MUMTAZ YUSUF OF SRI LANKA,
SAID OF THE ENGLAND TOURING SIDE

So how's your wife, and my kids?

ROD MARSH TO IAN BOTHAM

Go and deflate yourself, you balloon.

DARYL CULLINAN TO SHANE WARNE

In England people do not speak to you unless they are firmly introduced with no hope of escape.

LEARIE CONSTANTINE OF THE WEST INDIES

Man for man, on paper, the Australian side stand out like dogs' balls.

GREG CHAPPELL, PREDICTING THE RESULT
OF THE 1994 ASHES SERIES

If the Poms win the toss and bat, keep the taxi running.

AUSTRALIAN BANNER

Tufnell! Can I borrow your brain? I'm building an idiot.

AUSTRALIAN BARRACKER TO PHIL TUFNELL

Passengers are reminded that they should be as quiet as possible on this trip because Mike Gatting is trying to catch up on his sleep.

FLIGHT ATTENDANT (GATTING, AS THE NEW ENGLAND
CAPTAIN, HAD ARRIVED LATE FOR PLAY IN
MELBOURNE AFTER HE HAD OVERSLEPT)

There was a strange, white laundry bag sitting in the bedroom on my arrival at the Menzies at Rialto, Melbourne. On further inspection it revealed its contents: a life-sized doll's head, with a very large open mouth attached to an ingenious pumping device. Phil, it transpired, had won the W**ker of the Series award.

FRANCES EDMONDS ON HER HUSBAND

First the convicts, then the rabbits and now Botham.

AUSTRALIA BANNER

You know a few Afrikaans swear words. Have a go
at him.

IAN BOTHAM, TO ALLAN LAMB, OF KEPLER WESSELS

They're capital winners out here, but I'm afraid that
I cannot apply the same adjective to them as losers.

LORD HARRIS

It'll be all right if Dennis [Lillee] gets the wickets.
But if he doesn't the knockers will say, 'Silly old
bastard.'

JEFF THOMSON ON LILLEE'S COMEBACK IN 1988

He could never make up his mind whether to call
heads or tails.

RAY ILLINGWORTH ON TED DEXTER

Fast bowlers are bully boys. They dish it out but they can't take it.

BRIAN CLOSE

When I hear Colin bowl de bounces, I get vex. Two bounces an over OK, but when he bowl five I get vex bad. I tell him, what happen if he hit batsman and he fall dead on de spot?

COLIN CROFT'S MOTHER DURING AN
ENGLAND TOUR OF THE WEST INDIES

When tha's laikin' wi' Fred, tha's not laikin' wi' a soft ball, tha knows.

FRED TRUEMAN ON HIMSELF ('LAIKING' IS A
YORKSHIRE TERM FOR 'PLAYING')

Do you wish to prefer charges?

POLICE OFFICER IN A HOSPITAL TO SUNIL WETTIMUNY,
WHO WAS INJURED AND SAID, 'JEFF THOMSON DID IT.'

[Derek] Pringle goes out looking like Worzel Gummidge with a borrowed untucked shirt, half-mast trousers six inches too short and no socks to cover up his hairy shins . . .

GRAHAM GOOCH ON PRINGLE'S BORROWED KIT

His biggest problem was an identity crisis. He wanted people to look up to him but he didn't know who he really was.

IAN BOTHAM ON PETER ROEBUCK

The Julie Andrews of cricket.

PETER ROEBUCK ON JOHN BARCLAY

One of the few men you would back to get past a
Lord's gateman with nothing more than an icy stare.

MARTIN JOHNSON ON PETER WILLEY

He takes an alternative view just for the hell of it.

GRAHAM GOOCH ON DEREK PRINGLE

Watching [Peter] Roebuck was like being at a
requiem mass.

JIM LAKER, AFTER SOME SLOW SCORING

On the boys from overseas

With national pride at stake, competition has always been fierce among Test-match cricketers; in particular between the 'Aussies' and the 'Pommies'. This selection of quotations highlights the intense rivalry between various international teams and players, giving examples of the insults traded between them and the insightful comments on each other's strengths and weaknesses.

I don't suppose I can call you a lucky bleeder when you've got three hundred and forty-seven.

ANGUS FRASER, DURING BRIAN LARA'S
RECORD-BREAKING INNINGS OF 375 IN 1994

Until we can breed seven-foot monsters willing to break bones and shatter faces, we cannot compete against these threatening West Indians.

DAVID FRITH

Ashes to ashes, dust to dust – if Thomson don't get ya, Lillee must.

SYDNEY TELEGRAPH CARTOON CAPTION

Don't bowl him bad balls – he hits the *good* ones for fours.

MICHAEL KASPROWICZ ON THE SKILLS
OF SACHIN TENDULKAR

I hate bowling at you. I'm not as good at hitting a moving target.

DENNIS LILLEE TO
DEREK RANDALL
(AFTER A HIGH
SCORE)

They've always had a lot of talent, a lot of good players, but they're like eleven women. You know, they're all scratching each other's eyes out.

IAN BOTHAM ON
PAKISTANI PLAYERS

Australians will not tolerate class distinction in sport.

J. H. FINGLETON

All Australians are an uneducated and unruly mob.

DOUGLAS JARDINE

A cricket tour in Australia would be the most delightful period in your life – if you were deaf.

HAROLD LARWOOD

If I've to bowl to Sachin [Tendulkar], I'll bowl with my helmet on. He hits the ball so hard.

DENNIS LILLEE

The Aussies try to present a tough-guy image, but this present generation are a bunch of sissies.

TONY GREIG IN 1996

If the countless columns written about him were placed end to end, they would stretch, on a still day, from the pavilion end at Puckapunyal, and would reach beyond the bounds of credibility.

RAY ROBINSON ON DON BRADMAN

He destroys bowlers nicely.

BOB WOOLMER ON A BRIAN LARA
RECORD-BREAKING INNINGS

He won't be great until he stops being a perfectionist.

IAN BOTHAM ON MARTIN CROWE

In cricketing terms, Graeme Pollock is a sadist.

EDDIE BARLOW

A corpse with pads on.

A BRITISH JOURNALIST ON AUSTRALIAN BILL LAWRY

[Allan] Border is a walnut: hard to crack and without much to please the eye.

PETER ROEBUCK

The mincing run-up resembles someone in high heels and a panty girdle chasing after a bus.

MARTIN JOHNSON ON MERV HUGHES

To call a crowd 'a crowd' in Jamaica is a misnomer. It should be called a mob . . . these people still belong to the jungles and forests instead of a civilized society.

SUNIL GAVASKAR ON INDIA'S 1976 TOUR
OF THE WEST INDIES

I was interested to hear Michael Holding say that
Curtly [Ambrose] is still learning. I hope he doesn't
learn too much more.

ALLAN BORDER, AFTER AMBROSE HAD JUST
DEMOLISHED SEVEN WICKETS FOR ONE RUN

I don't know why they bother to put the stumps out.
None of those buggers are trying to hit them.

GRAEME FOWLER ON WEST INDIAN FAST BOWLERS

There's no batsman on earth who goes out to meet
Dennis Lillee or Jeff Thomson with a smile.

CLIVE LLOYD

I've never felt it more likely that we should see
someone killed.

JOHN WOODCOCK IN *THE TIMES* ON
WEST INDIAN FAST BOWLERS

Playing against a team with Ian Chappell as captain turns a cricket match into gang warfare.

MIKE BREARLEY

The only time an Australian walks is when his car runs out of petrol.

BARRY RICHARDS OF SOUTH AFRICA

They must have fallen asleep in a greenhouse with their feet in a growbag.

FRED TRUEMAN ON THE SIZE OF
WEST INDIAN FAST BOWLERS

Dustin Hoffman and some Aussie bowlers in the act of appealing.

DARYL CULLINAN, A SOUTH AFRICAN BATSMAN,
ASKED WHO HIS FAVOURITE ACTORS WERE

If all living things in India are incarnations, [Sunil] Gavaskar is technical orthodoxy made flesh.

SCYLD BERRY

Javed Miandad looks like a wild man with a face you might spot crouched behind rocks in ambush along the Khyber.

MIKE LANGLEY ON PAKISTAN'S JAVED MIANDAD DURING
EARLY-NINETIES BALL-TAMPERING ROW

[Dilhara] Fernando is a renowned hooker.

JONATHAN AGNEW

Srikkanth's a vegetarian. If he swallows a fly he'll be in trouble.

SUNIL GAVASKAR

You'll never die of a stroke, Mackay.

A FAN JEERING KEN 'SLASHER' MACKAY'S SLOW BATTING

Deep Dasgupta is not a wicketkeeper, he is a goalkeeper. He must be given a free transfer to Manchester United.

NAVJOT SIDHU

There's no ruddy best ball to bowl at the Don.

BILL VOCE ON DONALD BRADMAN

The taste of blood stimulated the Australians; they are terrible when they feel a grip on their prey, almost carnivorous.

NEVILLE CARDUS

On the men in white coats

Depending on what he does or doesn't claim to have seen in the field of play, an umpire will either be a cricketer's saviour or his nemesis on the pitch. Criticism of umpiring standards has always been rife in the cricketing world – never more so since the introduction of the third umpire in Test-match cricket in the early 1990s – which is humorously reflected in the majority of the following quotations.

It is amazing to think that there should have been two such complete idiots standing so close to one another at a given moment.

C. P. FOLEY ON UMPIRES

It is possible, if the truth were known, that more county matches have been won by umpires than either batsmen or bowlers.

E. V. LUCAS

The third umpires should be changed as often as nappies and for the same reason.

Navjot Sidhu

Our team should sleep well during lunch time and while the third umpire makes his decision to win more matches.

Deva Gowda, former Indian Prime Minister

Every umpire should be given a computer or a laptop.

Chandrababu Naidu, India's Chief Minister

[Third umpire] Eddie Nichols is a man who cannot find his own buttocks with his two hands.

Navjot Sidhu, after Nichols had ruled
Shivnarine Chanderpaul not out

Umpire Bucknor is a lingering death merchant.

Henry Blofeld bemoans Steve Bucknor's
slow decision-making

I learned more in my first year as an umpire than in all the previous twenty-six years of playing the game.

E. J. SMITH

If anyone were to ask us the question 'what class of useful men receive most abuse and least thanks for their service?' we should, without hesitation, reply, 'Cricket umpires'.

A. G. STEEL

Mike Gatting used some filthy language to the umpire, and let me tell you: some of the less filthy words are 'bastard' and 'son of a bitch' and so on. No one has a right to abuse umpires.

SAFDAR BUTT, PAKISTAN CRICKET BOARD PRESIDENT

Ee, lad, tha's a bit of a character. Tha could 'ave bin a great comedian thissen.

ALBERT MODLEY, COMEDIAN, TO DICKIE BIRD,
UMPIRE (WHO WAS A CHARACTER)

He arrived on earth from the Planet Looney to become the best and fairest of all umpires. Great bloke, completely bonkers.

IAN BOTHAM ON DICKIE BIRD

I don't understand why, in a democratic society, where government and all the accepted standards in every walk of life are being questioned, umpires should be immune.

ASIF IQBAL

Most umpires have good memories. If you stuff them once, they'll stuff you good and proper in the end.

ALAN OAKMAN

The only acceptable form of dissent is a dirty look – and we don't like that.

ENGLAND TEST UMPIRE

Comments on the commentators

While the TV commentary team imparts a myriad of fascinating insights to the viewer, from the opening over until close of play, on the radio the listener relies solely on the commentators' descriptive prowess to help visualize the action on the pitch, but often hears a great many other interesting details besides. Of Britain's best-loved cricket commentators, John Arlott and Brian Johnston stand unrivalled: perhaps the most famously quoted and now most sadly missed.

In [John] Arlott's day the radio team had a centre of gravity; in the age of [Brian] Johnston a centre of levity.

RUSSELL DAVIES ON JOHNSTON'S DEATH IN 1994

Halfway between the Ten Commandments and Enid Blyton.

J. J. WARR ON E. W. SWANTON'S CRICKET BROADCASTING

The commentary lost more than just [John] Arlott's unassuming gravitas. When he retired, the commentary team lost much of its humanity.

SIMON BARNES, AFTER ARLOTT'S DEATH IN 1991

My word! I know what the problems are. I've failed at everything.

JOHN ARLOTT ON HIS RETIREMENT

One viewer told me the other day that listening to my old mate Jim Laker and his new sidekick Bob Willis was better than taking two Mogadon.

FRED TRUEMAN, TALKING OF TV COMMENTATORS

He had, over half a century, perfected and personified that hardly definable English sound, the burble.

GODFREY SMITH, *SUNDAY TIMES*, ON BRIAN JOHNSTON

Probably the most celebrated British voice after Churchill's.

FRANK KEATING ON JOHN ARLOTT

A man with music-hall imagination.

JOHN ARLOTT ON BRIAN JOHNSTON

Exact, enthusiastic, prejudiced, amazingly visual, authoritative and friendly . . . he sounds like Uncle Tom Cobleigh reading Neville Cardus to the Indians.

DYLAN THOMAS ON JOHN ARLOTT'S COMMENTARY STYLE

It's the way they tell 'em

Out of the mouths of sports commentators, players and fans come all kinds of stuff and nonsense. One commentator in particular brings us some of the most satisfying quotes, and that's the lovable Henry ('Blowers') Blofeld, whose plummy tones can be heard on BBC Radio 4. We've honoured Blowers by giving him his own subsection at the end of this selection of assorted blunders and gaffes.

A brain scan revealed that Andrew Caddick is not suffering from stress fracture of the shin.

JOE SHELDON

Two balls remain.

DAVID GOWER (COMMENTATING AT A TEST MATCH) AFTER THE BATSMAN HAD BEEN HIT IN THE GROIN BY A BALL

I was once offered a Foster's from someone over the fence, but it was warmer and frothier than a Foster's.

BOB WILLIS

I'm very concerned for our middle order. We've already called on the immediate next people down, so who do you go to next? I've got a four-year-old son who might like a go.

KEN RUTHERFORD

If Srinath can bowl a little extra pace, it will make the ball come to the bat more faster.

KRIS SRIKKANTH

I'm working very hard on this relaxation business.

GRAEME WOOD

Well, he's bravely going to carry on, but he doesn't look too good. One ball left.

BRIAN JOHNSTON (COMMENTATING AT AN ENGLAND–NEW ZEALAND TEST) AFTER BATSMAN GLENN TURNER WAS HIT IN THE GROIN BY A BALL

I was on ninety-nine . . . I got really scared. I pooped my pants, missed the next ball and was bowled.

BRAD HODGES

Another day, another dolour.

MATTHEW ENGEL, WITH ENGLAND IN THE WEST INDIES IN 1985–6

There's Anil Kumble. We're looking forward to seeing him bat, he's a very useful bowler.

CRICKET COMMENTATOR

There is light at the end of the tunnel for India, but it's that of an oncoming train which will run them over.

NAVJOT SIDHU

There are twenty-five thousand people here today and they are all here to watch the cricket.

LOUIS KARPUS

The Indians are finding the gaps like a pin in a haystack.

NAVJOT SIDHU

That was a magnificent #@*^!% shot!

BILL LAWRY (MORE EXCITABLE THAN USUAL)

The Zimbabwe–England tie is very important from India's point of view because, irrespective of the outcome there, India have to beat England.

KRIS SRIKKANTH

One who doesn't throw the dice can never expect to score a six.

NAVJOT SIDHU

Omar Henry hit one or two boundaries in his seven.

NIC COLLINS

Lloyd's talking to his slippers.

TONY GREIG, REFERRING TO MEN IN THE SLIPS

Look at Siddons. He's ready to throw like a panther.

KIM HUGHES

Sri Lankan score is running like an Indian taxi meter.

NAVJOT SIDHU

One of the hardest things is to take a caught-and-bowled off your own bowling.

MIKE HAYSAM

One needs to understand that Test cricket is Test cricket and one-day cricket is one-day cricket.

KRIS SRIKKANTH

It's his second finger, technically his third.

CHRISTOPHER MARTIN-JENKINS

It is important for Pakistan to take wickets if they are going to make big inroads into this Australian batting line-up.

MAX WALKER

I get a few strange looks when I use the hotel laundry. They're used to washing shirts and socks, but not too many have been asked to clean a panther's head!

THE BARMY ARMY'S KEVIN THAME, ON WEARING HIS PINK PANTHER COSTUME IN THE SWELTERING BANGLADESHI HEAT DURING ENGLAND'S TEST MATCHES

Marshall's bowling with his head.

TONY GREIG

Now Botham, with a chance to put everything that has gone before behind him.

TONY COZIER

For every winner, there has to be a loser in these games.

TONY GREIG

Fast bowlers are quick, even at the end of the day. Just watch this . . . admittedly it's in slow motion.

IAN CHAPPELL

Chappell just stood on his feet and smashed it to the boundary.

JIM MAXWELL

The pitch is as dead as a dodo.

NAVJOT SIDHU

There is Neil Harvey, with his legs wide open, waiting for a tickle.

BRIAN JOHNSTON

As a result, Tasmania picks up two valuable points, not that they are of any value now. The match has already been decided.

GERRY COLLINS

Two short legs, one of them being [Nasser] Hussein himself.

JONATHAN AGNEW

As a captain not in a good form, Sourav Ganguly should realize that he should play well.

KRIS SRIKKANTH

Alderman knows that he's either going to get a wicket, or he isn't.

STEVE BRENKLEY

The ball whizzes past like a bumble bee and the Indians are in the sea.

NAVJOT SIDHU

Steve Waugh might do a bit of slather and whack.

RICHIE BENAUD

He went through a bad patch where he couldn't bat his eyelids.

MIKE SELVEY

Ganguly played what can only be described as a cow shot.

CHRISTOPHER MARTIN-JENKINS

Patel took it down on his knees in front of slip.

JONATHAN AGNEW

. . . if you can get somebody out before they get in . . .

GEOFF BOYCOTT

That's the second time Maher has been bitten – beaten.

ROD KILNER

Border was facing a four-paced prong attack.

DAVE RENNEBERG

I condone anyone who tampers with the ball.
ALLAN LAMB BEING MRS MALAPROP

I've seen batting all over the world. And in other countries, too.

KEITH MILLER

All England want now is a wicket, first and foremost, and then five more.
CHRISTOPHER MARTIN-JENKINS

On the outfield, hundreds of small boys are playing with their balls.

REX ALSTON

Botham has two short legs, one of them square.

BRIAN JOHNSTON

A very small crowd here today. I can count the people on one hand. Can't be more than thirty.

MICHAEL ABRAHAMSON

It's tough for a natural hooker to give it up.

IAN CHAPPELL

I didn't drop my pants and moon the crowd: I just went a little bit over the top. I carried on like a pork chop, but the bottom line was I didn't do anything wrong.

SHANE WARNE ON HIS 1997 BALCONY CELEBRATIONS
AFTER A WIN AT TRENT BRIDGE

Newspapers are only good enough for wrapping up fish and chips. They are the pits.

MARTIN CROWE

I doubt if many of my contemporaries, especially the older ones, did many exercises. I have often tried to picture [Godfrey] Evans and [Denis] Compton doing press-ups in the outfield before the day's play, but so far have failed miserably.

PETER MAY

What a magnificent shot! No, he's out.

TONY GREIG

Butcher plays this off the black foot.

BRIAN JOHNSTON

When I've made off-the-cuff remarks it's been as much as anything because the atmosphere at press conferences has been so poisonous, so thoroughly unpleasant, that I've tried to lighten it a bit.

TED DEXTER ON RESIGNING IN 1993

The Queen's Park Oval, exactly as its name suggests – absolutely round.

TONY COZIER

Strangely, in slow-motion replay, the ball seemed to hang in the air for even longer.

DAVID ACFIELD

The sound of the ball hitting the batsman's skull was music to my ears.

JEFF THOMSON

Bloody Botham Bastard Bugger Mother Evil Satanist KGB.

SPITTING IMAGE'S TAKE ON RUPERT MURDOCH'S
HAILING A *SUN* 'EXCLUSIVE' ON IAN BOTHAM

A unique occasion, really – a repeat of Melbourne in 1987.

JIM LAKER ON BBC TV

G'day, howya going?
DENNIS LILLEE'S 1972 ADDRESS AT LORD'S TO THE QUEEN

Sorry, Skipper, a leopard can't change his stripes.
LENNY PASCOE, APOLOGIZING FOR BOWLING BOUNCERS

His throw went absolutely nowhere near where it was going.

RICHIE BENAUD

That was a tremendous six: the ball was still in the air as it went over the boundary.

FRED TRUEMAN

Alderman knows that he's either going to get a wicket, or he isn't.

STEVE BRENKLEY

. . . and Marshall throws his head to his hands.

CHRISTOPHER MARTIN-JENKINS

He's no mean slouch as a bowler.

MIKE DENNESS

The pattern of the match is certainly swaying towards Kent.

TOM GRAVENEY

Even Downton couldn't get down high enough for that.

RICHIE BENAUD

There are good one-day players, there are good Test players, and vice versa.

TREVOR BAILEY

That black cloud is coming from the direction the wind is blowing; now the wind is coming from where the black cloud is.

RAY ILLINGWORTH

And he's got the guts to score runs when the crunch is down.

JOHN MURRAY

He caught it like shelling peas.

FRED TRUEMAN

No captain with all the hindsight in the world can predict how the wicket is going to play.

TREVOR BAILEY

The Sri Lankan team have lost their heads, literally.

GAMINI GOONASENA

It's a truism to say that there's been a change in the weather here at Trent Bridge this morning.

JIM LAKER

For any budding cricketers listening, do you have any superstitious routines before an innings, like putting one pad on first and then the other one?

TONY LEWIS

We owe some gratitude to Gatting and Lamb, who breathed some life into a corpse which had nearly expired.

TREVOR BAILEY

It was a good tour to break my teeth in.

BERNARD THOMAS

That slow-motion replay doesn't show how fast the ball was travelling.

RICHIE BENAUD

That's what cricket is all about. Two batsmen pitting their wits against one another.

FRED TRUEMAN

The bowler's Holding, the batsman's Willey.

BRIAN JOHNSTON

I don't think he expected it, and that's what caught him unawares.

TREVOR BAILEY

Well, everyone is enjoying this except Vic Marks, and I think he's enjoying himself.

DON MOSEY

Anyone foolish enough to predict the outcome of this match is a fool.

FRED TRUEMAN

I don't know if this is his highest score in the John Player League. If not, this is his highest score.

ROBERT HUDSON

The first time you face up to a googly you're going to be in trouble if you've never faced one before.

TREVOR BAILEY

He'll certainly want to start by getting off the mark.

DON MOSEY

I was surprised that Geoff Howarth won the toss.

JIM LAKER

People started calling me 'Fiery' because 'Fiery' rhymes with Fred, just like 'Typhoon' rhymes with Tyson.

FRED TRUEMAN

That's a remarkable catch by Yardley, specially as the ball quite literally rolled along the ground towrds him

MIKE DENNESS

Unless something happens that we can't predict, I don't think a lot will happen.

FRED TRUEMAN

And Jajeda is dijappointed . . . Jadeja is ji . . . da . . . I'll come again, Jajeda . . . okay Jadeja looks downcast.

TONY GREIG

Then there was that dark horse with the golden arm, Mudassar Nazar.

TREVOR BAILEY

So that's 57 runs needed by Hampshire in 11 overs – and it doesn't need a calculator to tell you that the run rate required is 5.1818.

NORMAN DEMESQUITA

And a sedentary seagull flies by.

BRIAN JOHNSTON

In the back of Hughes's mind must be the thought
that he will dance down the piss and mitch one.

TONY GREIG

Joel Garner, he pockets them for breakfast.

FRED TRUEMAN

And Ian Greig's on eight, including two fours.

JIM LAKER

I think if you've got a safe pair of hands, you've got
a safe pair of hands.

TOM GRAVENEY

He didn't quite manage to get his leg over.

JONATHAN AGNEW, AFTER IAN BOTHAM HAD
LOST HIS BALANCE AND TRIED, WITHOUT SUCCESS,
TO STEP OVER THE WICKET

On the first day, Logie decided to chance his arm,
and it came off.

TREVOR BAILEY

He's usually a good puller – but he couldn't get it up
that time.

RICHIE BENAUD

An interesting morning, full of interest.

JIM LAKER

It's been very slow and dull day, but it hasn't been boring. It's been a good, entertaining day's cricket.

TONY BENNEWORTH

I think we are all slightly down in the dumps after another loss. We may be in the wrong sign or something. Venus may be in the wrong juxtaposition with somewhere else.

TED DEXTER, EXCUSING A TEST LOSS

There is a widely held and quite erroneous belief that cricket is just another game.

DUKE OF EDINBURGH

Welcome to Leicester, where the captain Ray Illingworth has just relieved himself at the pavilion end.

BRIAN JOHNSTON

There was a slight interruption there for athletics.

RICHIE BENAUD ON TV, REFERRING TO A STREAKER AT LORD'S

Glenn McGrath joins Craig McDermott and Paul Reiffel in a three-ponged prace attack.

TIM GAVEL

Laird has been brought in to stand in the corner of the circle.

RICHIE BENAUD

Welcome to Worcester, where we've just seen Barry Richards hit one of Basil D'Oliveira's balls clean out of the ground.

BRIAN JOHNSTON

If you go in with two fast bowlers and one breaks down, you're left two short.

BOB MASSIE

The sight of Bright holds no fright for Wright . . . and the riposte: That's right!

JIM MAXWELL

It's funny kind of month, October. For the really keen cricket fan, it's when you realize that your wife left you in May.

DENNIS NORDEN

It was close for Zaheer. Lawson threw his hands in the air and Marsh threw his head in the air.

JACK POTTER

Yorkshire were 232 all out, Hutton ill. No, I'm sorry, Hutton 111.

JOHN SNAGGE

And there's the George Headley Stand, named after George Headley.

TREVOR QUIRK, DURING A TEST AT BRIDGETOWN

Marshall's bowling with his head.

TONY GREIG

BLOW BY BLOW BY BLOWERS

And that nearly took Mongia's nose off. If there was a drip on the end of his nose it'll be on the pitch now.

Thorpe just nibbles that, nurdles it down to third man.

. . . a seagull trotting around at long off.

Hick scratches around like an old hen in the crease there.

It's awfully uncomfortable to have McGrath up your sleeve, isn't it?

And a white seagull flies overhead, a very white seagull. I wonder which washing powder it uses.

. . . a rather posthumous appeal.

It's a catch he would have caught ninety-nine times out of a thousand.

In the rear, the small diminutive figure of Shoaif Mohammed, who can't be much taller or shorter than he is.

That action of Sehwag was quite inexplickers.
[said after Virender Sehwag had just been given LBW]

There goes twinkle toes [Sachin] Tendulkar. His legs were running almost faster than he was.

And it gets excitinger and excitinger.

A bumble bee has just come to have a look at us through the window. They're lovely buzzy things, I rather like bumble bees – bumble bees and ladybirds.

Radio 4 listeners you are back after the most exciting shipping forecast there's ever been, except you didn't hear it because it was happening here at Lord's. [Blowers was bemoaning the fact that an exciting wicket had been taken while the shipping forecast was interrupting commentary]

Excitement all around the ground. If this were a bottle of champagne the top would blow off at any moment.

He's permanently hung up his jockstrap.
[on a cricketer's retirement from the game]

We had a winking seagull the other day. You don't often see a seagull wink.

No one's paying a blind bit of notice at the moment. A helicopter flies over. It's been rather good for helicopters.

A huge seagull flies over our heads and away. Is that another helicopter? No, I think it's an aeroplane.

Umpire Tiffin signals a rather airy leg bye there.

Another plane coming in rather slowly – it ought to waggle its wings a bit but that would upset the passengers.

Off the pads

Well, we had to think of something to call this section rather than boring old 'Miscellaneous', but, hey, what's in a name? It's given us a chance to throw in some more quotes that don't quite fit into the other categories.

They said to me at the Oval, 'Come and see our new bowling machine.' 'Bowling machine?' I said. 'I used to *be* the bowling machine.'

ALEC BEDSER

Well, to be honest, the fackin' facker's fackin' facked.

JOHN EMBUREY (TALKING ABOUT INJURIES)

Concentration is sometimes mistaken for grumpiness.

MIKE ATHERTON

The dogs, birds and cats on the cricket field should be protected.

MENAKA GANDHI

It's very rewarding being a pain in the arse.

JACK RUSSELL, ENGLAND WICKETKEEPER,
AFTER HE'D SAVED THE JOHANNESBURG TEST
AGAINST SOUTH AFRICA IN 1996

Statistics are like miniskirts, they reveal more than what they hide.

NAVJOT SIDHU

If Zimbabwe shock Australia by scoring 275 runs, Australia will shock Zimbabwe by scoring 276 runs.

KRIS SRIKKANTH

Pakistan is the sort of place every man should send his mother-in-law, for a month, with all expenses paid.

IAN BOTHAM

If you ever captain Australia, don't do it like a Victorian.

VIC RICHARDSON TO HIS GRANDSON IAN CHAPPELL

If there is cricket in heaven, let us also pray that there will be rain.

ARTHUR MARSHALL

That ball went so high it could have got an air hostess down with it.

NAVJOT SIDHU

I and my family are horrified they should have
called this team the Graces without asking us. We
are not being beastly to gays, but they could have
found out about the Grace family. We are the Graces
and we object to them using our family name.

> MORNY GRACE, WIDOW OF W. G. GRACE'S
> GREAT-GRANDSON HAMISH GRACE, ON AN ALL-GAY
> TEAM WHO CALL THEMSELVES THE GRACES

If you lads don't back off, I'll appeal for bad light!

> FRED TRUEMAN COMPLAINS OF TOO MANY CLOSE-IN
> FIELDERS WHILE HE'S TRYING TO BAT

I'm allergic to taking wickets – it makes me come
out in a rash.

> MICHAEL LANGLEY EXCUSES A SLOW
> START TO THE SEASON

When you're a batter and a bowler, you enjoy
yourself twice as much.

GEORGE HIRST, A YORKSHIRE ALL-ROUNDER

The gap between bat and pad is so much that I
would have driven a car through it!

NAVJOT SIDHU

As in life so in death lies a bat of renown,
Slain by a lorry (three ton);
His innings is over, his bat is laid down;
To the end a poor judge of a run.

CRICKETER'S GRAVESTONE IN ENGLAND

You know you're in Melbourne when you're walking
through the park and you see someone kicking the
footy with cricket pads on.

HUNG LE

I suppose if you don't play in gloom up here, you
never play at all.

ALAN KNOTT ON OLD TRAFFORD

Steady, boys. Put down a canary first.

J. B. EVANS ABOUT TO GO DOWN INTO THE VISITORS'
BASEMENT DRESSING ROOM AT TAUNTON

Bloody Derby! What a way to go!

JONATHAN AGNEW ON HIS LAST MATCH BEFORE
RETIREMENT FROM THE GAME

I think I could write a sort of Egon Ronay guide to
casualty departments – a kind of *Good Hospital
Guide*.

A MUCH-INJURED GRAHAME CLINTON

I didn't need anyone to motivate me. Playing for
England was all I needed.

ALEC BEDSER

You lead in May, and I shall catch you in June.

PHILIP MEAD TO TEAMMATES DURING PRE-SEASON
NETS PRACTICE IN THE 1920S

I'll have quite a rugged countenance by the time I'm
finished.

MIKE BREARLEY, AFTER BEING HIT ON THE NOSE

In England an unpredictable climate would appear
to have made both officials and players more ready
to accept a drawn game than is the case, say, in
Australia.

ALLEN SYNGE

Helmets are unfair to bowlers.

VIV RICHARDS

When I see a young man who has an expensive and pretty hairdo, I have doubts as to his ability to reach Test standard.

TED DEXTER

You have to clap yourself on at the WACA.

GARY GILMOUR

Wickets are like wives – you never know which way they will turn!

NAVJOT SIDHU

There's no evidence that people who use weapons for sport are any more dangerous than people who use golf clubs or tennis rackets or cricket bats.

DUKE OF EDINBURGH

Isn't it rather odd that, despite all the clouts and swipes, there are, year in and year out, so few pavilion windows broken?

E. H. D. SEWELL

The way Indian wickets are falling reminds me of the cycle stand at Rajendra Talkies in Patiala: one falls and everything else falls!

NAVJOT SIDHU

Forget the White Rhino, Save the Poms!

I can't bat, can't bowl and can't field these days. I've every chance of being picked for England.

RAY EAST

Each word in a bar, each whisper in a lift, each phrase in a press conference, each indiscreet stroke on the pitch, is whacked on the back page, replayed on the TV screens and tut-tutted on the radio.

MARK NICHOLAS

We have the worst press in the cricketing world. Hardly any of them could write a proper cricket report, even if their editors wanted that . . . which they don't.

ALLAN LAMB

You buggers have been lampooning and harpooning me.

TED DEXTER TO REPORTERS

My ghost is writing rubbish.

ENGLAND PLAYER DURING A 1986 WEST INDIES TOUR

But my dear chap, it's the spirit of the thing that counts. Often when I quoted a player he may not have literally said those things. But he'd have liked to.

NEVILLE CARDUS

When I tap the pitch with my bat, someone else taps back.

PETER WALKER ON PLAYING IN WELSH
MINING COUNTRY IN 1967

I absolutely insist that all my boys should be in bed before breakfast.

COLIN INGLEBY-MACKENZIE IN 1961,
THEN HAMPSHIRE CAPTAIN

No disrespect, but playing for Surrey Seconds against Sussex this week in front of a few dogs and coffin-dodgers is quite a different experience to playing before packed houses at the Oval, Headingley and Old Trafford.

ALISTAIR BROWN

I always thought that the best way to contain a batsman was to get him back into the pavilion.

ALEC BEDSER

You can see the moon. How far do you *want* to see?

ARTHUR JEPSON, UMPIRE, WHO HAD JUST REFUSED AN
APPEAL ON THE GROUNDS OF BAD LIGHT

Good players don't need 'em. Bad players aren't worth it.

BRIAN 'TONKER' TAYLOR ON PHYSIOTHERAPISTS

Certainly I am told that you can play cricket better after a marijuana cigarette than after a couple of pints of beer.

LORD WIGODER, OLD BAILEY JUDGE

It was like getting out of jail.

CHRIS ADAMS ON HIS DEPARTURE FROM
DERBYSHIRE IN 1998

The three Hs: Hack, Hooligan and Hallucination
must apply to the British media.

ASIAN TIMES DURING THE BALL-TAMPERING ROW IN 1992

I may be black, but I know who my parents are.

VIV RICHARDS TO A RACIST HECKLER

This series could be to cricket's box office what
Attack of the Killer Tomatoes was to the cinema
industry.

QUEENSLAND OFFICIAL ON POOR TICKET SALES

What do you think this is, a f**king tea party? No,
you can't have a f**king glass of water. You can
f**king wait like the rest of us.

ALLAN BORDER TO ROBIN SMITH

If they call me a 'Pommie bastard' or something, I'll
say, 'You're right, mate. Now buy me a beer.'

PHIL TUFNELL ON AUSTRALIAN PLAYERS

In my day, fifty-eight beers between London and
Sydney would have virtually classified you as a
teetotaller.

IAN CHAPPELL ON DAVID BOON, WHO HAD DRUNK
FIFTY-EIGHT BEERS BECAUSE HE WAS AFRAID OF FLYING

Where's the groundsman's hut? If I had a rifle, I'd shoot him now.

BILL O'REILLY, SPIN BOWLER, NOT LIKING THE WICKET

The aim of English Test cricket is, in fact, mainly to beat Australia.

JIM LAKER

All I have to do is bowl loopy-doopies to them and they commit suicide.

PHIL TUFNELL ON WEST INDIAN BATSMEN

I'd thrown them off the top of the pavilion. Mind, I'm a fair man. I'd give them a fifty–fifty chance. I'd have Keith Fletcher underneath trying to catch them.

FRED TRUEMAN ON WICKET SABOTEURS (FLETCHER WAS NOT MUCH THOUGHT OF AS A CATCHER)

I never watch TV replays. If I did, I'd go crazy.

DICKIE BIRD, UMPIRE

Here's three ha'pence. Buy a paper and find out the score.

ALEX SKELDING, UMPIRE, DISAGREEING WITH THE
SCOREBOARD OPERATOR

Hey, hey, hey, hey! I'm f**king talking to you. Come here, come here, come here, come here . . . Do that again and you're on the next plane home, son . . . What was that? You f**king test me and you'll see.

ALLAN BORDER, AUSTRALIAN CAPTAIN,
ARGUING WITH CRAIG MCDERMOTT

As I'm walking back I think maybe I'll bowl a googly.
Then, as I run in, I think, no, I'll bowl a leg-spinner.
Then, do you know, just as I prepare to bowl, I
decide it'll be a googly after all. And then, as I let go
of the ball, I say, 'Sod it – I'll bowl a top-spinner.'

BHAGWAT CHANDRASEKHAR

I enjoy hitting a batsman more than getting him out.
I like to see blood on the pitch. And I've been
training on whisky.

JEFF THOMSON

I don't mind seeing blood on the pitch.

JASON GILLESPIE, AUSTRALIAN FAST BOWLER

He'd better not bite that – it's the finger I give 'em
all out with.

DICKIE BIRD, AFTER BEING ATTACKED BY A PARROT

None of us likes fast bowling, but some of us don't
let on.

MAURICE LEYLAND

Wouldn't it be better if I got in the fridge?

QASIM OMAR, RECEIVING ICE TREATMENT FOR BRUISES

I'm working very hard on this relaxation business.

GRAEME WOOD

It's not hard to look at the way my life has developed and realize that there are things I should not have done.

DOMINIC CORK

Maybe I should smile a bit more and do the old high fives and be Mr Bouncy; raise the profile and have a nice spin-off contrast for wearing something or other. But that's not me. I look like I do on the field because what I do is knackering.

ANGUS FRASER

When I'm batting, I like to pretend I'm a West Indian.

DARREN GOUGH

It's no pose, man. I'm f**king babooned.
Look at my eyes.

BEN HOLLIOAKE EXPLAINING THE NEED FOR DARK GLASSES ON A TOUR OF SRI LANKA IN 1998

I'm an instinctive player, but at the moment I'm thinking too much and have become a gibbering wreck.

ROBIN SMITH

The Establishment seem to want my ability but not me.

GEOFF BOYCOTT

You don't know three-quarters of seven-eighths of sod all.

DAVID BAIRSTOW, OFTEN SAID TO JOURNALISTS

I know I look a totally miserable sod on television. I wish I didn't, but there you are.

GRAHAM GOOCH

This champagne's all right, but the blackcurrant jam tastes of fish.

DEREK RANDALL, EATING CAVIAR DURING A TOUR OF INDIA

Gel is more macho than a hair band.

WASIM AKRAM, WHO WANTED TO KEEP
HIS HAIR OUT OF HIS EYES

You don't need a helmet facing Waqar [Younis] so much as a steel toe-cap.

SIMON HUGHES

You don't want to be taking them pills: you want to get some good Tetley's down you.

DAVID BAIRSTOW RECOMMENDING TETLEY'S BITTER TO A
YORKSHIRE BOWLER WHO WASN'T DOING TOO WELL

I just have to make a suggestion these days and it's interpreted as being antagonistic.

PHIL EDMONDS

I still have the butterflies, but I now have them flying in formation.

MARK TAYLOR

Thoughts on the game

Many of cricket's more highfalutin quotations come from those who pontificate on the game itself. Some famous names are there, whether it's those of old such as Rudyard Kipling and Arthur Conan Doyle, or the cricketers and commentators of today.

Ninety-nine per cent of cricket manuals belong in the dustbin.

IAN BOTHAM, AS HE INTRODUCED HIS OWN

I was brought up to believe that cricket is the most important activity in men's lives, the most important thread in the fabric of the cosmos.

BERNARD HOLLOWOOD

If anyone had told me I was one day destined to make a reputation as a writer upon cricket, I should have felt hurt.

NEVILLE CARDUS

The one-day game, the idea of never-dull, action-packed cricket with all the homey atmosphere of speedway racing and the amenities of a Wimpy bar, is Mickey Mouse cricket, but nobody will mention it.

STANLEY REYNOLDS

Casting the ball at three straight sticks and defending the same with a fourth.

RUDYARD KIPLING (QUOTED BY SIR NEVILLE CARDUS)

To this day I have never been present at a cricket match though this odd activity is hard to escape when you have a TV and a family that thinks God wears white flannels.

JAMES CAMERON

To stand upright during so many hours of an extreme heat; to take a violent exercise without any need; to run deliberately a grave danger not less than that which one is obliged to encounter on a field of battle – all this is folly of the most profound. I cannot believe that there is really some pleasure at all in it.

ANATOLE GONJON

If the French *noblesse* had been capable of playing cricket with their peasants, their châteaux would never have been burned.

G. M. TREVELYAN

Cricket is no excuse for ignorance.

BARRY PEROWNE

One-day cricket has debased the currency, both of great finishes and of adjectives to describe them.

MATTHEW ENGEL

Cricket as a passion is distinctly contagious.

DAVID FRITH

Cricket is quite a gentle, harmless game, but he is a lucky man who has not to sweat some blood before he's done with it.

J. C. SNAITH

There can be raw pain and bleeding where so many thousands see the inevitable ups and downs of only a game.

C. L. R. JAMES

I have thumbed through the MCC coaching manual and found that no such stroke exists.

PETER MAY, THEN CHAIR OF THE SELECTORS, ON IAN BOTHAM'S REVERSE SWEEP

It is a brave pastime, a game for soldiers, for each tries to strike the other with the ball, and it is but a small stick with which you ward it off.

SIR ARTHUR CONAN DOYLE

I had devoted too much of my life to this utterly irrational game. I would chuck the whole thing and take to Strindberg for amusement.

A. A. THOMSON

O, Wind, if Membership Card comes, can Spring be far behind?

ROY HATTERSLEY

I've known grown men to lose their appetite for breakfast at the mere mention of rain on the radio.

NICO CRAVEN

Oh, I am so glad you have begun to take an interest in cricket. It is simply a social necessity in England.

SAID BY MRS CROCKER TO HER HUSBAND BINGLEY, IN P. G. WODEHOUSE'S *PICCADILLY JIM*

Too much cricket will kill cricketers before they are ready to be killed.

MIKE GATTING

It has become tougher, more brutal, more combative, and is a game where the letter has taken over from the spirit of the law.

HENRY BLOFELD

The cricket world, surely, is as crazy and as inconsistent as the outside one.

JACK FINGLETON

If a cricketer wants safety and security then let him go into a bank and work. If he's going to play cricket then let him enjoy the game and entertain the public.

MARGARET HUGHES

Whatever the authorities may say to the contrary, cricket is nowadays increasingly run by the players both on and off the field.

HENRY BLOFELD

Sharp practice in our national game is probably a good deal more common than most Englishmen would care to admit.

HERBERT FARJEON

The allure of a cricket ball flying through space is too simple for words, inexplicable but equally irrefutable, making the great gulf between the level-tempered pleasure of the expert and the involuntary and unrestrained joy of the mere human being.

T. C. F. PRITTIE

Although village cricket is loosely built around the laws of cricket, its adherence to them is subject to wide interpretations, and subtle variations, and is more characteristic in the breach than in the observance.

ROBERT HOLLES

But after all it's not the winning that matters, is it? Or is it? It's – to coin a word – the amenities that count: the smell of the dandelions, the puff of the pipe, the click of the bat, the rain on the neck, the chill down the spine, the slow, exquisite coming on of sunset and dinner and rheumatism.

ALISTAIR COOKE

A game of cricket is a variety show which, on a good day, will put many different talents on view: magicians of spin and masters of pace, acrobatic close-fielders and, in the outfield, athletes with prodigious throwing arms.

ALLEN SYNGE

'Cricket,' he once remarked, 'was intended to be played between twenty-two sportsmen for their own pleasure; it was never meant to be the vehicle for international competition, huge crowds and headline news – otherwise it wouldn't have been given a code of laws with such gaps as you could drive through with a coach and horses.'

B. H. LYON (QUOTED BY JOHN ARLOTT)

The best of games, yes, it is still that, at least for those who have taken to it and respect it (not 'love' it: I distrust anyone who says he 'loves' cricket).

ALAN GIBSON

You see, cricket had something against it, rather like tennis, which few played. It was played better by the English.

TONY LEWIS

> Cricket is the queerest game,
> Every stroke is just the same,
> Merely whacking at a ball;
> Nothing else to see at all,
> Then there comes some big surprise
> When I chance to close my eyes.

ANONYMOUS

This game preys on doubt. It is a precarious game. Form, luck, confidence are transitory things. It's never easy to work out why they have so inexplicably deserted you.

PETER ROEBUCK

Even if it is foolish to pray about cricket, there is no doubt that many of us succumb, especially when we are young.

ALAN GIBSON

I have always liked the idea of cricket. A day sitting in a deckchair in the sun, preferably with at least one similarly inclined companion to while away the longueurs between overs, seems to me a very civilized way of spending one's time. If the game becomes exciting, so much the better, though anyone who thinks that cricket can or should be consistently exciting fails, I think, to understand the game's appeal.

TIM HEALD

At times I do get despondent with what I see on the field. The players don't look very happy, there aren't many characters around and many see it as a job of work. If they only knew that, in a few years' time when their careers are over, they'll miss the game and perhaps then they'll wish they'd enjoyed it more.

E. J. SMITH

We want to admire the stars for what they are as well as for what they do – which is why the exhibitionist antics of a few in recent times, giving the worst of examples to the young watchers on television, are so particularly abhorrent.

E. W. SWANTON

The Golden Age is behind us. But then it always was.

BENNY GREEN

A gentle game, cricket . . . Not much strain or stress, a pleasant afternoon in green pastures, basking in the warm rays of the sun. A time of ease, a time to unwind from the cares of life. A time for reflection, a time to recite the poems of one's youth, a time to revel in the pleasing sound of leather on helmet.

PETER ROEBUCK

Alcohol and the psychological blow, when retirement came, of descending into obscurity after having been a respected and well-known figure, were the undoing of many.

CHRISTOPHER MARTIN-JENKINS

Cricketers have become slaves of fashion, reflecting life in a much-changed Britain. The embarrassing habit of embracing each other whenever a wicket falls is the most jarring. In my time bowlers expected wickets and took them in their stride.

E. M. WELLINGS

[Dennis] Lillee said in a television interview, quite clinically illustrating his point, that there were certain parts of the body which he aimed to hit when bowling short to a batsman.

MIKE DENNESS

My definition of a foreigner is someone who doesn't understand cricket.

ANTHONY COUCH

I see them in foul dug-outs, gnawed by rats,
And in the ruined trenches, lashed by rain,
Dreaming of things they did with balls and bats.

SIEGFRIED SASSOON

Has there ever been a game in the history of the
world so lovingly waffled over as cricket?

STANLEY REYNOLDS

Don't practise on an opponent's ground before
match begins. This can only give them confidence.

SIR J. M. BARRIE

Some are born with silver spoons in their mouths. I was born in Pudsey. You can't be luckier than that if you want to play cricket.

RAY ILLINGWORTH

A fast bowler may well say that he does not want to maim batsmen, but he knows that every time he delivers that ball there is a chance of causing serious injury.

MIKE DENNESS

I'd like to think that I haven't got any weaknesses except chocolate and a bad back.

GRAEME HICK

You have a bat with which to defend yourself. What more do you want? I will answer: I want a tin hat, a chest protector, a fencing mask and – and a revolver for the bowler.

M. D. LYON

What's money got to do with it? Why can't people just sit there and enjoy the spectacle in front of them? Why do they have to spoil it for everyone else?

GRAEME HICK

The ball hit him in the mouth, driving his lips through his teeth, and in writing him a letter of sympathy I could not help adding that I should advise him in future not to put his head where his bat ought to be.

LORD HARRIS

He played his cricket on the heath,
The pitch was full of bumps:
A fast ball hit him in the teeth,
The dentist drew the stumps.

ANONYMOUS

A Test match is there to be fought and won, not
played with in an amused and off-hand manner.

RONALD MASON

I don't think cricket fans really want to see a lot of
people being hit on the head or going down with
broken ribs.

MIKE DENNESS

Even the Yorkshire Ripper got a fair trial.

GEOFF BOYCOTT, AFTER HE'D FAILED TO
GET THE ENGLAND CAPTAINCY

If something's not done to excess, it's hardly worth
doing.

PETER ROEBUCK

You bastards have been out to get me since I arrived.
All you Aussies are a bunch of hicks who don't
know the first thing about cricket.

IAN BOTHAM TO JOURNALISTS, AFTER BEING
SACKED BY QUEENSLAND IN 1988

When you win the toss, bat. If you are in doubt, think about it, then bat. If you have very big doubts, consult a colleague – then bat.

W. G. GRACE

A few cracks starting to appear on the pitch. We've seen a lot of cracks here at the WACA in the last few years, some at least ten to twelve centimetres wide.

RICHIE BENAUD

Cricket – a game which the English, not being a spiritual people, have invented to give themselves some conception of eternity.

LORD MANCROFT

Basically, it's just a whole bunch of blokes standing around scratching themselves.

KATHY LETTE

We have a great opportunity for the rebirth of English cricket . . . the creation of one happy and successful family from the village green to the Test arena.

A. C. SMITH, RETIRING AS CHIEF EXECUTIVE OF THE TEST AND COUNTY CRICKET BOARD AS IT GAVE WAY TO THE ENGLISH CRICKET BOARD IN 1996

Bowling which does not get men out, like batting which brings no runs to the score, is an art abused.

A. E. KNIGHT

The cover drive is the most beautiful stroke in batsmanship. Does that throw any light on why I am a self-admitted lover of all things British and traditional?

COLIN COWDREY

Bowling is the most important thing in the game. It's the brainiest part of cricket.

H. M. HERMAN

Mastering boredom is the chief requirement of the cricketer.

DAVID OLDHAM

A cricket ground is no place to separate the good from the bad. It's us and them.

CARYL PHILLIPS

Cricket grounds are like seaside resorts. They come alive in the summer with the sunshine and the deck chairs and the bunting and the bands, but like seaside resorts I find them oddly appealing out of season when they are empty and windswept.

TIM HEALD

Lord's cricket, cricket straight out of Debrett.

NEVILLE CARDUS

International cricket is fiercely competitive – dog eat dog with big dogs.

MALCOLM SPEED

Is there any sex in it?

PETER SELLERS ON CRICKET

There are many human beings, a trifle vague as to its origins and functions, who believe that it [Lord's] is firmly associated with our peerage rather than just plain Mr Lord.

JOHN MARSHALL

Test cricket is not a light-hearted business, especially that between England and Australia.

DONALD BRADMAN

Important facts from Galactic history, number one: The night sky over the planet Krikkit is the least interesting sight in the entire Universe.

DOUGLAS ADAMS (*LIFE, THE UNIVERSE, AND EVERYTHING*)

Cricket? It civilizes people and creates good gentlemen. I want everyone to play cricket . . . I want ours to be a nation of gentlemen.

ROBERT MUGABE

To make watching cricket more fun and much more popular.

ENGLAND'S BARMY ARMY MISSION STATEMENT

Cricket is like sex films. They relieve frustration and tension.

LINDA LOVELACE

Cricket is organized loafing.

WILLIAM TEMPLE, ARCHBISHOP OF CANTERBURY

Cricket is the easiest sport in the world to take over. Nobody bothered to pay the players what they were worth.

KERRY PACKER IN 1977

You don't know how tough it is out here!

BILL ALEXANDER, AFTER A BALL HAD SHOT
STRAIGHT BETWEEN HIS LEGS AT POINT

Cricket has got to be the dreariest game in the world. If it wasn't for the fact that I've just been bored to death, the prospect of having to sit through yet another interminable game would force me to end it all.

GRAFFITI AT CRICKET GROUND

Cricket does keep those boys off the street.

CARMEL SHUTE (PARTNER OF KEN NORLING)

We've got football, baseball, basketball. You've got cricket – baseball on Valium.

ROBIN WILLIAMS

If there is a game that attracts the half-baked theorists more than cricket, I've yet to hear of it.

FRED TRUEMAN

I reckon cricket would be better if it were played from only one end.

BILL ALEXANDER, WHO DIDN'T LIKE HAVING
TO WALK BETWEEN OVERS

They might as well bulldoze Lord's. I'll never go there again.

UNNAMED, NOT TO SAY MISOGYNISTIC, MCC MEMBER,
AFTER A VOTE TO ADMIT WOMEN TO THE FAMOUS CLUB

Batsmen wear so much protection these days that I mostly identify them from their posteriors.

BRIAN JOHNSTON

The amateur tradition in cricket has the same defects off the field as on.

DEREK BIRLEY

Gone were the days when finger-licking spinners could follow a rainbow and expect to find a sticky wicket glued to the ground for their benefit.

NICO CRAVEN

Even Test match bowling all over the world is so basic that it may be said to have gone right through the floor into the bargain basement.

LEARIE CONSTANTINE

You cannot prosper as a batsman unless you have a fundamentally correct technique.

VIV RICHARDS

Around the most illustrious of opening partnerships there lingers a romantic flavour.

E. W. SWANTON

There are easier things in the world than stopping a fast yorker.

P. G. WODEHOUSE

If a batsman is obliged to wait with his pads on for more than half an hour he is normally reduced to the condition of frogspawn, and this state will accompany him on the field of play and last for at least a couple of overs, which are seldom survived.

ROBERT HOLLES ON VILLAGE CRICKET

Scores didn't count, and they don't with some of the great batsmen. It's what you do and how you do it that matters.

DAL STIVENS

Batting is an unrivalled variety show in itself.

ALLEN SYNGE

The margin of error between middle and edge of a cricket bat is, after all, only two inches. That is a truth which never enters a batsman's mind when he is in form; when he is off, it can become an obsessive hazard.

JOHN ARLOTT

Like all cricket devotees I have many, many times shared with all around me that infectious, 'breathless hush' tension as a batsman, however well set, however self-possessed, has to face up to the obligation of scoring that hundredth run.

BEN TRAVERS

When the batsmen were not actually beaten by the spin they were out making desperate shots for fear of what the ball might do next.

DAVID LACEY

Cricket is a most precarious profession; it is called a team game but, in fact, no one is so lonely as a batsman facing a bowler supported by ten fieldsmen and observed by two umpires to ensure that his error does not go unpunished.

JOHN ARLOTT

Half the joy of cricket is playing the innings over again in your mind afterwards.

CHRISTOPHER HOLLIS

Everyone must from time to time bow to the needs of the team, whether it be by taking risks or visiting the sponsor's tent.

PETER ROEBUCK

Cricket is a game, a game of social enjoyment. It is not a fit subject for an inquest, which must be, or at any rate should be, a very serious affair.

PHILIP TREVOR

Cricket is a subtle game. In form and appearance it can be gentle, even idyllic, yet violence is always there.

MIHIR BOSE

English cricket is an irrelevance on and off the ground, and that is not the ramblings of an Anglophobe. It is a statement of fact.

MIKE COWARD, AUSTRALIAN CRICKET WRITER

Why should I buy cricket? Nobody watches it.

GREG DYKE, WHEN HE WAS CHAIR OF ITV NETWORK SPORTS COMMITTEE IN 1988

You plan your cricket like a war, but play it like a party game.

TONY LEWIS

As preparation for a Test match, the domestic game is the equivalent of training for the Olympic marathon by taking the dog for a walk.

MARTIN JOHNSON, *THE INDEPENDENT*

Without overseas players, the English county game would be dead.

RICHARD HADLEE IN 1985

The rush of sponsorship in the early seventies did for English cricket, because it propped up the knackered counties and the weak players who should have been consigned to the history of the game.

GREG CHAPPELL

We have far too much to do in the game these days. You need one eye up your backside.

ARTHUR JEPSON ON FIELDING CIRCLES
IN ONE-DAY CRICKET

There is no way we will allow Test cricket to die. Test cricket is like classical music; limited-overs cricket is like modern commercial music.

JAGMOHAN DALMIYA

A Test match is like a painting. A one-day match is like a Rolf Harris painting.

IAN CHAPPELL

One-day cricket is entertaining all right, but not entirely a sport. Once sport consciously tries to be entertaining, it sets off on the short but dangerous road that leads to the Worldwide Wrestling Federation.

SIMON BARNES, *THE TIMES*

How much simpler it is to swat a fly with a rolled-up newspaper than with a telephone directory.

DENIS COMPTON, ON HIS DESIRE TO RETURN
TO THE USE OF LIGHTER BATS

Massive bats, helmets, big gloves . . . it's rather like sending Nureyev onto the stage at Covent Garden to dance the *Nutcracker Suite* in sea-fisherman's waders.

DENIS COMPTON, TALKING ABOUT MODERN BATTING

Cricket must be the only business where you can make more money in one day than you can in three.

PAT GIBSON, *DAILY EXPRESS*, ON THE ONE-DAY GAME

Throw down some sawdust, everybody put on top hats and red noses, and you've got the John Player League.

BRIAN CLOSE ON THE SUNDAY FORTY-OVERS GAME

To me the best preparation for batting, bowling and fielding was batting, bowling and fielding.

PETER MAY

In an England cricket eleven, the flesh may be of the South, but the bone is of the North, and the backbone is Yorkshire.

LEN HUTTON

Cricket needs brightening up a bit. My solution is to let the players drink at the beginning of the game, not after. It always works in our picnic matches.

PAUL HOGAN

The history of Pakistani cricket is one of nepotism, inefficiency, corruption and constant bickering.

IMRAN KHAN

Up, breakfast, stretch, practise, play, bathe, bar, steak, bed. Same company, day in, day out.

IAN BOTHAM ON TOURING

It's Test cricket; it's tough. If you want an easy game, take up netball.

STEVE WAUGH

I never play cricket. It requires one to assume such indecent postures.

OSCAR WILDE

He is but a weak-kneed cricketer who in his heart approves of the umpires' decisions.

R. C. ROBERTSON-GLASGOW

I don't know what these fellows are doing, but whatever they are doing, they sure are doing it well.

PETE SAMPRAS ON WATCHING BRIAN LARA
AND CURTLY AMBROSE AT LORD'S

Say, when do they begin?

GROUCHO MARX, WHILE WATCHING A
CRICKET MATCH AT LORD'S

If they want pitches that do bugger all, that's easy. If they want pitches that are dangerous, that's easy, too . . . If the TCCB [Test and County Cricket Board] aren't careful, they'll frighten groundsmen into being responsible for producing exactly the sort of cricket they used to moan about before.

RON ALLSOPP, GROUNDSMAN

Too much crap cricket on crap wickets.

TOM MOODY, AUSTRALIAN BATSMAN,
ON ENGLISH CRICKET

Cricket teams have often suffered from captains who have arrived, done queer things, departed and been forgotten.

R. C. ROBERTSON-GLASGOW

A captain can do nothing for his side other than win the toss.

K. J. KEY

A public-relations officer, agricultural consultant, psychiatrist, accountant, nursemaid and diplomat.

DOUG INSOLE ON CAPTAINS

The bloody ball should never be changed until the string starts to fray from it and the four segments of it start to come adrift.

BILL O'REILLY

Poor old Googly! It has been subjected to ridicule, abuse, contempt, incredulity, and survived them all.

B. J. T. BOSANQUET, WHO INVENTED IT

It's all a matter of inches – those between your ears.

ARTHUR MILTON ON PLAYING SPIN

You must rinse your hands in the chamberpot every day. The urine hardens them wonderfully.

HERBERT STRUDWICK PROVIDES WICKETKEEPING ADVICE

Captaincy is ninety per cent luck and ten per cent skill. But don't try it without that ten per cent.

RICHIE BENAUD

I try to hit a batsman in the ribcage when I bowl a purposeful bouncer, and I want it to hurt so much that the batsman doesn't want to face me any more.

DENNIS LILLEE

Remember, with those speedsters bowling at ninety-five miles per hour, cricket can kill.

AUSTRALIAN TV ADVERT FOR THE PACKER CIRCUS

'Cricket' used to be a synonym for honourable conduct. It is now becoming a synonym for brute force. Is it not time that respected leaders in all countries spoke out?

LORD BROCKWAY, CRITICIZING SHORT-PITCHED FAST BOWLING IN A LETTER TO THE *GUARDIAN*

I regard an over as having six bullets in a gun. I use those bullets strategically, to manipulate the batsman into a certain position or state of mind, so that I can eliminate him.

RICHARD HADLEE

To bowl fast is to revel in the glad animal action, to thrill in physical power and to enjoy a certain sneaking feeling of superiority over the mortals who play the game.

FRANK TYSON

Batting is a major trial before an eleven-man jury.

RICHIE BENAUD

The thicker you are, the better your chances of becoming a quick bowler.

STEWART STOREY

Ninety per cent of cricket is played in the mind.

RICHARD HADLEE (GIVING ADVICE)

It's hard work making batting look effortless.

DAVID GOWER

What do I think of the reverse sweep? It's like Manchester United getting a penalty and Bryan Robson taking it with his head.

DAVID LLOYD

It's always a good idea to aim the first ball right here at the bowler's head. They don't like it. It rattles 'em.

CHARLIE MACARTNEY

West Indies minus Ambrose = Poms.

BANNER AT 1997 PERTH TEST

All Michael O'Mara titles are available by post from:

Bookpost, PO Box 29, Douglas, Isle of Man, IM99 1BQ

Credit cards accepted.
Telephone: 01624 677237
Fax: 01624 670923
Email: bookshop@enterprise.net
Internet: www.bookpost.co.uk

Free postage and packing in the UK.

Other Michael O'Mara Humour titles:

All Men Are Bastards – ISBN 1-85479-387-X pb £3.99
The Book of Urban Legends – ISBN 1-85479-932-0 pb £3.99
Born for the Job – ISBN 1-84317-099-X pb £5.99
The Complete Book of Farting – ISBN 1-85479-440-X pb £4.99
Complete Crap – ISBN 1-85479-313-6 pb £3.99
The Ultimate Book of Farting – ISBN 1-85479-596-1 hb £5.99
The Ultimate Insult – ISBN 1-85479-288-1 pb £5.99
Wicked Cockney Rhyming Slang – ISBN 1-85479-386-1 pb £3.99
Wicked Geordie English – ISBN 1-85479-342-X pb £3.99
Wicked Scouse English – ISBN 1-84317-006-X pb £3.99
The Wicked Wit of Jane Austen – ISBN 1-85479-652-6 hb £9.99
The Wicked Wit of Winston Churchill – ISBN 1-85479-529-5 hb £9.99
The Wicked Wit of Oscar Wilde – ISBN 1-85479-542-2 hb £9.99
The World's Stupidest Criminals – ISBN 1-85479-879-0 pb £3.99
The World's Stupidest Graffiti – ISBN 1-85479-876-6 pb £3.99
The World's Stupidest Laws – ISBN 1-85479-549-X pb £3.99
The World's Stupidest Men – ISBN 1-85479-508-2 pb £3.99
The World's Stupidest Signs – ISBN 1-85479-555-4 pb £3.99
More of the World's Stupidest Signs – ISBN 1-84317-032-9 pb £4.99
The World's Stupidest Last Words – ISBN 1-84317-021-3 pb £4.99
The World's Stupidest Inventions – ISBN 1-84317-036-1 pb £5.99
The World's Stupidest Instructions – ISBN 1-84317-078-7 pb £4.99
The World's Stupidest Sporting Screw-Ups – ISBN 1-84317-039-6 pb £4.99
Shite's Unoriginal Miscellany – ISBN 1-84317-064-7 hb £9.99
Football: It's A Funny Old Game – ISBN 1-84317-091-4 pb £4.99